DATE DUE

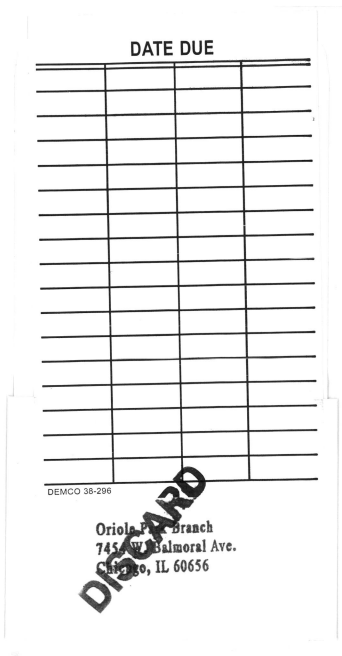

Tiger Woods

by Jonatha A. Brown

Reading consultant: Susan Nations, M.Ed., author/literacy coach/consultant

WEEKLY WR READER®
EARLY LEARNING LIBRARY

Please visit our web site at: www.earlyliteracy.cc
For a free color catalog describing Weekly Reader® Early Learning Library's list
of high-quality books, call 1-877-445-5824 (USA) or 1-800-387-3178 (Canada).
Weekly Reader® Early Learning Library's fax: (414) 336-0164.

Library of Congress Cataloging-in-Publication Data

Brown, Jonatha A.
    Tiger Woods / by Jonatha A. Brown.
        p. cm. — (People to know)
    Includes bibliographical references and index.
    ISBN 0-8368-4313-4 (lib. bdg.)
    ISBN 0-8368-4320-7 (softcover)
    1. Woods, Tiger—Juvenile literature. 2. Golfers—United States—Biography—Juvenile literature.
I. Raatma, Lucia. Tiger Woods. II. Title. III. People to know (Milwaukee, Wis.)
GV964.W66B76 2004
796.352'092—dc22
    [B]   2004045132

This edition first published in 2005 by
Weekly Reader® Early Learning Library
330 West Olive Street, Suite 100
Milwaukee, WI 53212 USA

Based on *Tiger Woods* (Trailblazers of the Modern World series) by Lucia Raatma
Editor: JoAnn Early Macken
Designer: Scott M. Krall
Picture researcher: Diane Laska-Swanke

Photo credits: Cover, title, pp. 5, 16 © J. D. Cuban/Getty Images; pp. 4, 8 © Jamie Squire/Getty Images;
p. 7 © Gary Newkirk/Getty Images; p. 9 © Alan Levenson/CORBIS; p. 10 © Ken Levine/Getty Images; p. 12
© Patrick Murphy-Racey/Getty Images; p. 13 © Rusty Jarrett/Getty Images; p. 15 © Mark Perlstein/Time Life
Pictures/Getty Images; p. 17 © Jeff Mitchell/Reuters; p. 20 © Logan Mock-Bunting/Getty Images

Printed in the United States of America

1 2 3 4 5 6 7 8 9 08 07 06 05 04

Table of Contents

Words that appear in the glossary are printed in **boldface**
type the first time they occur in the text.

Chapter 1: Tiger Cub

Tiger Woods is one of the best golfers in the world.

Tiger Woods was born on December 30, 1975. He was a beautiful baby with soft, brown skin and dark eyes. His real first name was Eldrick, but no one called him that. He was always known as Tiger.

Tiger's parents both had mixed racial backgrounds. Tiger and his parents lived in Cypress, California. Most people there were white. Some of them did not want to have neighbors with brown skin. They wanted the Woods family to leave. But Tiger's parents did not leave. They stayed in Cypress to raise their little boy.

Tiger's father loves golf, too. Here he and Tiger are wrapped up in a game.

Tiger's father liked to play golf. Sometimes he was not allowed to play golf where white people played. He did not like that, but he still loved golf. Mr. Woods often practiced his golf **swing** in the garage. He liked to bring his baby son along to watch. They both had fun. Tiger sat in his high chair and giggled and laughed. Meanwhile, Mr. Woods practiced.

An Early Start

Little Tiger wanted to hit golf balls, too. One day he picked up a big golf club. He swung it just like his father did. He could barely stand up, but he hit the ball! Tiger was proud and happy. His father was very surprised.

Soon the little boy learned to walk. He went with his father to play golf. They walked around the golf courses together. Tiger wanted to play, too, but his father's clubs were twice his size. Mr. Woods soon solved that problem. He bought a set of tiny clubs for his son.

Now Tiger could play golf. He practiced and practiced with the little clubs. His swing was very good. By the time he was three years old, he played golf as well as many adults. Tiger was amazing!

The more Tiger practiced, the better he played.

Chapter 2: School Days, Golf Days

Tiger started school when he was five years old. His first day was not easy. Some older white kids

Tiger's mother is very proud of him.

called him names and beat him up. They did not know Tiger, but they did not like him just because he had brown skin. The little boy was hurt and confused.

Tiger went back to school. He learned to **ignore** people who did not like the color of his skin. He worked hard and got good grades. He still loved to play golf, but his parents said that school must come first. He could not play golf until he had finished his homework.

Mr. Woods was Tiger's first coach.

First Things First

Mr. and Mrs. Woods knew that their young son was a very good golfer. They did not want his skill and success to spoil him. That is why they put school first. They also taught Tiger that he must always be polite, on the golf course and off.

A few years went by, and Tiger kept playing golf. When he was eight years old, he played in a

Young Tiger played golf for fun. But he also played to win.

big **tournament** for kids. He was the youngest player on the course. No one thought he had a chance of winning. But they were wrong. To everyone's surprise, he won.

Learning to Play

Tiger Woods was on his way. He played in more tournaments, and he won quite a few of them. Golfers young and old started talking about him. Some thought he would grow up to be famous.

As a teenager, Tiger played well. But he did not win every tournament. Sometimes he got nervous. Sometimes he did not play his best. Tiger learned a lot from those times. He learned not to blame others for his own mistakes. He learned to behave well even when he lost. He learned to smile and **congratulate** the winner.

Chapter 3: College and Beyond

After high school, Tiger went to Stanford University in California. There he had to work hard to do well in his classes. He also kept working on his golf game. By 1994, he was one of the best young players in the country. He had much to be proud of. But Tiger was not **satisfied**. He wanted to play even better.

Tiger went to Stanford University. He played on the golf team there.

In 1994, Tiger won the U.S. Amateur Championship. He was the youngest player ever to win that tournament.

Tiger was very busy. He went to classes and studied a lot. He was like most other students in that way. But he also played golf all over the country. He often had to rush from one place to another.

Turning Pro

After two years, he began to feel tired. Going to college was a full-time job. Playing golf could be a full-time job, too. Tiger began to think he could not do both. He talked to his parents. They agreed that he had a big decision to make.

By this time, Tiger had been playing golf for many years. He had won many times. He had earned many prizes. But Tiger had never played as a **professional**. That meant he had never won a cash prize in a golf tournament.

The best golfers are professionals. When they win, they earn money. When they lose, they do not. Tiger decided to turn pro. He would give up college and play golf for money.

Tiger turned pro in 1996. He made a hole in one at his first pro tournament, the Greater Milwaukee Open.

Chapter 4: Professional Golfer

This is Tiger in his first year as a pro. He is lining up a shot.

Tiger turned pro in 1996. He was only twenty years old. Some golfers said he was too young. Some said he could not hold his own against the best. But Tiger and his parents thought he was ready.

Winning is sweet!
Tiger has won
many big trophies
like this.

In his first pro tournament, he did not do well. He ended up in sixtieth place. But Tiger got better quickly. In his fourth **competition**, he placed third. And then, in his fifth tournament, he beat all the other players and ended up in first place. Tiger had won a pro tournament!

He played well for the next few months. He did not win every time, but he always placed near the top. Other golfers said Tiger was the best new player of the year. *Sports Illustrated* magazine named him Sportsman of the Year. Tiger was very proud.

Success on and off the Course

Years have gone by, and Tiger Woods still stands out. He has won most of the important golf competitions at least once. He is recognized as one of the greatest golfers of our time. Because he is so popular, many companies want him to help sell their products. He is often seen in commercials. In 2003, Tiger Woods was honored by his **peers** for the fifth year in a row. The players on the Professional Golfers' Association (PGA) Tour named him Player of the Year.

Breaking Records

Tiger Woods has broken many records. He started when he was very young. He was the youngest player ever to win the U.S. Junior Amateur Championship. He was the youngest player ever to win the U.S. Amateur Championship.

The Grand Slam is a series of four golf tournaments. Tiger Woods was the youngest player ever to win all four. Then he became the only player ever to win all four in a row. Tiger Woods is still breaking records.

Tiger stands out in another way, too. Most other pro golfers are white. Tiger is not. His success has proven that skin color doesn't matter in golf. In his spare time, he teaches golf to boys and girls of all colors and backgrounds. He shows them that golf can be a great sport for anyone who loves the game.

Tiger likes his fans. He also likes to help young golfers by giving them tips.

The Tiger Woods Foundation

Tiger Woods knows how to reach his goals. He wants to pass on what he has learned. He wants kids to be responsible and still have fun. He shows them how to be honest and play by the rules. He started the Tiger Woods Foundation to help. Tiger Woods invests his own time and money to do good for others.

The Tiger Woods Foundation helps raise money for good causes. It tells parents to be involved in their children's lives. It gives money to programs for children and families. It offers golf clinics for kids. It gives **scholarships** to students. It helps kids pursue their dream goals.

Glossary

competition — contest

congratulate — to show pleasure to someone for his or her success

ignore — to take no notice of

peers — equals

professional — in sports, someone who plays to win money

satisfied — contented or pleased

scholarships — money given to pay for education

swing — a stroke made with a sweeping arm movement

tournament — a series of games or contests

For More Information

Books

Tiger Woods. All Aboard Reading (series). Andrew Gutelle (Grosset & Dunlap)

Tiger Woods. Real People (series). Pamela Walker (Children's Press)

Tiger Woods. Real-Life Reader Biography (series). John Albert Torres (Mitchell Lane)

Tiger Woods. Sports Heroes (series). Elizabeth Sirimarco (Capstone)

Web Sites

Role Models on the Web: Tiger Woods
www.rolemodel.net/tiger/tiger.htm
Interesting information about Tiger's life and career

Tiger Woods's official web site
www.tigerwoods.com/splash/splash.sps
Lots of details and statistics on Tiger's career

Index

About the Author

Jonatha A. Brown has written several books for children. She lives in Phoenix, Arizona, with her husband and two dogs. If you happen to come by when she isn't at home working on a book, she's probably out riding or visiting with one of her horses. She may be gone for quite a while, so you'd better come back later.